Barkitecture

Explore the World of Innovative and Sustainable Pet Architecture

Joshua Thomasson

ROCK
POINT

↑ Ms. Darla is our unofficial mascot of the Triangle Barkitecture event and a local favorite. She always brings her signature smile and is the perfect advocate for all the love and joy a bully breed can bring.

This book is dedicated to pet rescue groups everywhere. Pet rescue is so much more than petting pups and kittens, cute photoshoots, and success stories of adopted pets. For every high, there are just as many lows, if not more. Pet rescue is hard work, and these dedicated individuals give so much of their time to those that can't fight for themselves, giving them a voice and a better future. Their work and stories inspire us to use pet architecture to raise awareness for their cause and put more pets in loving homes.

Contents

← **Pup Pawd (page 69)**

→ **Look who we caught sunbathing on The Bark Royal by The Bobbitt Group, Inc. (page 105).**

Introduction

This book tells the story of Barkitecture through our local event, Triangle Barkitecture—a custom pet architecture competition benefiting local animal rescues in the Research Triangle (Raleigh, Durham, and Chapel Hill) of North Carolina and beyond. The event is a celebration of creativity, compassion, and the special bond we share with our pets while supporting an important cause.

Barkitecture is not just about designing extraordinary structures for pets; it's about using the power of design to make a difference in our communities. Since its inception in 2019, Triangle Barkitecture has evolved from a small event into an annual tradition, donating more than $100,000 to local animal rescues. What started as a fun way to bring attention to the issue of pet homelessness has become a significant source of support for the organizations working tirelessly to find homes for adoptable pets.

Each year, local animal rescue groups were invited to the event where every build was auctioned off with all proceeds going to support our rescue partners. These rescues are also featured at the back of this book in Meet the Barkitects and Rescues (see page 134).

Our event would not be possible without the support of AIA Triangle, a

local chapter of the American Institute of Architects. AIA Triangle brings together architects and design professionals from across the region, advocating for the power of design to shape our community and the world around us. Through Triangle Barkitecture, we've been able to showcase the talent, ingenuity, and passion of our local architects and designers, each of whom blurs the lines between architecture and art, all in the name of a good cause.

We hope that this book will inspire you to not only dream big about future DIY projects but also spark ideas for creating spaces that show love for your pets. We also hope this inspires you to get involved. Whether it's through adoption, fostering, donating, or simply spreading the word, there are so many ways you can help support the local rescues that make events like Triangle Barkitecture possible. Every bit of support, big or small, makes a difference in the life of an animal waiting for their forever home.

Barkitecture is a testament to what happens when creativity meets compassion and design becomes a tool for change. We believe that together we can help build a future where every pet has a loving home, and maybe even a piece of Barkitecture to call their own.

Barkitecture Beginnings

It would be hard to forget the first day my dad brought Madison home. He was a curly, light brown and slightly untrusting cocker spaniel who had just lost his home and was unsure of this new space in which he found himself. The transition from low growls and side-eyes at the little human who sat on the floor trying to get his attention to curling up in bed and going on outdoor adventures was quite unexpected, but stands as a testament to the really special bond between a kid and his first true dog.

Although our pets cannot tell us what they want, or what they like, they leave a lasting impression that we take with us through life. For me, there's Maya's *aaa-woo*s greeting at the door and Shaggy's nervous cuddles during a thunderstorm. Savannah's wiggly butt when getting scratches, Muffin's unwavering patience to a clumsy child, and Cocoa's tendency to . . . nibble. Even now a passing thunderstorm or just the simple act of coming home after a long day at work still jogs these memories and the pets we could never forget.

In retrospect, the combination of being an only child in a small town and having an active imagination may or may not have always been the most relaxing thing for my pets growing up. When not playing with LEGO, some other ways I used to entertain my pets and me included backyard adventures—even though I'm sure my pets were content to lounge on the sofa. One of our favorite activities was playing in my tree fort, which was more in name only, as there were no actual trees in or around it: its raised floor was only accessible through a ladder and a bright yellow slide. Although it was not designed for them, it did not take long to find out that my dogs were innovative, and the slide quickly became a challenging way to access the tree fort. Over time, when having an outdoor playhouse eventually became less "cool," this fort became (what I did not know at the time) my very first barkitecture design—a new type of house for our pets to take breaks from the southern Virginia summertime heat. A simple, shingled gable roof with plywood sides painted forest green, it wasn't exactly the most beautiful design, but the pups didn't seem to mind (although I think they missed the slide).

Fast forward years later, and that same active imagination and love for solving creative challenges led me to architecture, a field I had no idea would eventually merge with my care and compassion for animals. Studio nights and work hours often kept me away from having pets of my own for far too long, but soon I found myself at the intersection of design and animal rescue, using my skills to positively impact the lives of pets in need.

Barkitecture may seem like an obvious idea now—the perfect combination of design and a love for pets—but like many promising ideas, the inspiration did not come overnight. There have been other events with similar ideas revolving around pet architecture, so we knew that ours needed to carve out its own identity and mission. It wasn't just about showcasing unique designs; it was about elevating the concept of barkitecture. Barkitecture would become not only a way for architects to tell stories of their own pets through design, but also a showcase of local adoptable pets and the stories of the rescues working to save them.

What began as an interest quickly evolved into organizing and building a committee into what it is today. Together, with a dedicated team, we created a major community event—one local designers and pet lovers look forward to each year.

Perhaps the most rewarding part of this journey has been my deeper involvement in and understanding of the world of pet rescue. Barkitecture has now partnered with over ten local rescue organizations,

giving them a platform to promote their mission, reach new audiences, and capture adorable photos of their adoptable pets interacting with the designs.

This path also led me to another first: welcoming a cat to my home, which quickly led to another, and . . . well let's just say I had many years of cat ownership to make up for and there are a lot of cats that need rescuing.

Scotch (short for Butterscotch) has what I'd describe as a very stereotypical cat personality, meaning you must work a little harder for his affection. But his adopted sister Stormi has never met a stranger and demands attention with headbutts, while Julip is the most toy-obsessed nocturnal cat you'd meet. I've quickly come to realize that finding the perfect pet architecture for them doesn't come off a store shelf—sometimes it just takes the right mind to craft that perfect space that will capture their attention and give them a restful place to still be near us.

Our cats (as well as Brandy, Goose, and Penelope) and dogs provide a lot of entertainment and inspiration when it comes to dreaming up big barkitecture ideas. The real creativity of barkitecture comes when thinking about creating pet architecture and spaces that suit these diverse pet families that don't just cater to a single cat or dog, but offer spaces for both, and you'll find some in this book.

Each structure at this event is a reminder of the pets who fill our lives with joy and the rescues working tirelessly to save them. Where every design is built with heart, welcome to *Barkitecture*.

A Tall Tail of Barkitecture

What's the first image that comes to mind when you hear "doghouse"? For many of us, it may conjure images of that classic structure with a red gabled roof and a beloved black-and-white beagle lying on top. But what if we took the same care and attention we apply to human architecture and translated it to our pets? That's the idea behind barkitecture, where creativity, function, and fun meet to create spaces where pets, not people, are the stars of the design.

Barkitecture, simply defined, is pet architecture, but unlike the traditional architecture client, the ideal barkitecture client can't necessarily communicate their wants, needs, or desires for their dream house—which, to be fair, is also sometimes true of our human clients as well. Enter the barkitect: the designer, dreamer, and full-time pet lover who bridges that gap, making sure your pet has a space just as tailored to their needs as any human dwelling. From clever storage solutions to luxurious lounging spots, barkitecture goes beyond aesthetics, blending functionality with a little bit of design flair.

HISTORY, BY A BARKITECT

Starting with barkitecture of today, let's take a quick look at the origins of pet design. A safe place for our faithful companions isn't exactly a new concept and has been around since the early days of human civilization.

Early hunter-gatherers discovered the benefits of having a dog by their side. This mutual relationship of survival and the domestication of wolves (which are now our pampered pups today) brought with it rudimentary shelters born of necessity and survival, but also laid the groundwork for the enduring relationship between humans and dogs.

A far cry from these primitive shelters, in ancient Egypt our feline friends found a place of somewhat divine status, with elaborate homes built and shared

with cat companions. There were even temples dedicated to them and Bastet, a catlike goddess of health, protection, and domesticity. Archaeological evidence has shown that some cats, much like their pharaohs, would be mummified and buried in tombs, to prepare them for their journey across the rainbow bridge. Though today's designs are less ornate, they reflect the same reverence we hold for our pets—and have less of that mummification!

As societies rose and evolved, so did the role of our pets. Perhaps beginning with the Romans, dogs became a symbol of status in society—and with that, the need for them to enjoy lavish and upscale accommodations in the villas they lived in and protected. Even as empires fell, the bond between our pets stood strong. Pet ownership became increasingly popular during

← Michelle Myers, from Freedom Ride Rescue, is telling her owner that she's not ready to leave the Ultimutt Hut (page 25) yet.

the Victorian era among the upper and middle classes with increasingly sophisticated doghouse designs to match their owners' tastes and favorite architectural styles—something that has made a bit of a comeback as we look for more ways to pamper our pets.

Fast-forward to the suburban boom in mid-twentieth-century America, and we see the emergence of the iconic prefabricated doghouse. To take advantage of the larger backyards in family homes where Fido roamed, simple, often mass-produced, slope-roofed houses became backyard staples and reflected a new era of convenience. While these homes were functional, they lacked the creativity and personalization that has come to define barkitecture today. As our connection to our pets has deepened, so has our desire to give them spaces that reflect their unique personalities.

PUP CULTURE AND BEYOND

Our love of pets has naturally infused its way into pop culture (or *pup* culture) and extended way beyond songs about hound dogs and mystery solving detectives with the munchies. With those lovable fictional characters also comes a need to construct spaces as iconic as them.

Perhaps the most recognizable doghouse is the red one that the iconic Charles Schulz created for the even more iconic character, Snoopy. Deceptively traditional and simple in its exterior design, this barkitecture opens up into an elaborate and luxurious interior—at least in Snoopy's imagination. The contrast of the two is a good metaphor for how we envision our pup's home and their ultimate wants and desires of comfort and entertainment.

Other famous characters have also had their time to shine as barkitects, although maybe without too much success. For example, Homer Simpson forgot to add a door to the doghouse he built for his dog, Santa's Little Helper, to enter or exit, so perhaps barkitecture should be left to the experts, or at least those with a little more patience and attention to detail.

Barkitecture has also invaded video games, giving creative minds the opportunity to play around and design doghouses for their virtual pets. *The Sims*, a long-running series, introduced a Cats & Dogs expansion pack that allows gamers to design custom homes for their video game family's pets—the ability to remove the ladder from your pup's pool not included.

Beyond the small screen, celebrities have also embraced the barkitecture trend. Media mogul and social star Paris Hilton famously commissioned a custom-designed two-story mansion for her pups, complete with a balcony, air conditioning, and furnishings fit for a king (or at least a very pampered pooch).

Swedish furniture giant IKEA has recently dipped their toes into the world of pets, introducing their very own pet line to go along with their beloved meatballs, college essentials, and signature sleek and modern style. They join a growing list of furniture suppliers riding the wave of stylish dwellings for pets that complement the rest of your home décor.

The rise of custom pet architecture in pop culture showcases how deeply our pets are woven into our daily lives, not only as companions but also as members of the family.

BARK TO THE FUTURE

As we look ahead, it's clear that the evolution of pet architecture and design is far from over. Our pets are integrated into our daily lives more than ever before. As their family roles continue to grow, so does the demand for a thoughtful, functional, and stylish space just for them.

From built-in nooks in living rooms to creative storage solutions for toys and treats, pet architecture is finding its way into mainstream home and building designs. Those prefab doghouses of yesteryear have now made way for more personalized spaces to reflect the bond dogs have with their owners, along with the owners' sense of style. Custom dog beds, stylish feeding stations, and even elaborate outdoor play areas are becoming more common as we embrace designs that cater to the needs of our loyal companions.

You're invited to go on a barkitectural journey that answers the question, *What is pet architecture?* To start, let's look through the lens of an architect and see how inspired design aims to create a better life for both our pets and us.

→ Size does not matter when it comes to Babushka Anya of Hope Animal Rescue, as seen here during a sampling of the Pawvilion by Gensler & SEAS (page 54).

Putting the Architecture in Barkitecture

Architecture is much more than just a job paying the bills so that our pups can have a better life. It's a unique profession that requires juggling a lot of specialized knowledge in different fields to ensure public safety, sustainability, and happy clients who see their vision come to life. The coordination among building codes, new technology, and client expectations makes for a challenging career—one rooted in problem-solving and innovation—using design to marry reality with the dream.

Humans spend most of their lives in the built environment, so why not make these the best possible spaces to ensure happy and healthier lives—and extend that same thought to our beloved furry companions?

There are not too many professions that touch the lives of so many people on a daily basis other than that of an architect. From the home you wake up in, to the building you work in, and all those you pass on a day-to-day basis, architects play a major role in shaping our lives and our future.

FAMOUS BARKITECTS

Some architects have reached the "starchitect" status—being considered a sort of celebrity in the design industry—and gaining a name of pop culture status. No matter how high architects rise for their groundbreaking and innovative designs, it hasn't stopped them from turning their attention to our furry companions.

Many high-profile architecture firms across the world have taken on the challenge of custom-designed pet abodes through design competitions and fundraisers. Major design firms like Zaha Hadid Architects joined dozens of other architects for the BowWow Haus in London to raise money for shelter pets. Their design, the Cloud, featured an elevated CNC-milled plywood nook to keep your pooch off the cold hard floor.

One of the most recognizable and well-known architects in history, Frank Lloyd Wright, could not resist the excitement that comes when designing for a pet. The architect of masterpieces such as

Fallingwater, the Guggenheim Museum, Taliesin, and the Robie House also took a detour into the world of pet architecture, being "commissioned" by a young boy after designing his family's home in Marin County, California. After the boy, Jim Berger, wrote to Wright, the master architect drew up plans reflective of his unique style to make the pup, Eddie, a very happy and stylish dream home. Today, the thought of having Frank Lloyd Wright agree to design your dog's new home may well be one of the greatest design flexes in the history of architecture.

While we can't all get a custom Wright or Hadid to add to our pet architecture collection, the idea that architecture should serve all—big and small—is at the heart of what barkitecture is about.

↑ **Can the BowWow House by RND Architects, PA (page 77) make this fluffy guy famous? I think the answer is yes!**

Even world-renowned and high-demand architects know that thoughtful and intentional design is for everyone.

THE NEXT BARKITECTS

Today, barkitecture continues to offer architects and designers a chance to step back from human-focused design, along with the complexities of building codes and zoning regulations. When designing barkitecture they have the opportunity to flex their creative muscles in new and innovative ways while embracing the challenge of designing spaces in which pets can thrive.

Barkitecture isn't just a fun distraction for architects; it's an opportunity to reconnect with the joy of creating something for the love of design. For many, it's a reminder of why they entered the profession in the first place: to innovate, problem solve, and bring joy through design. For others, it's a way to honor their pets, both past and present, and to craft designs that are inspired and influenced by the pets we love and share our lives with.

We're proud to introduce you to the next generation of barkitects—the dreamers, designers, and architects tasked with the challenge of what pet architecture can be. From whimsical play structures to sustainable interior furniture, these barkitecture designs push the boundaries of creativity and prove that no design is too small to have compassion and intent at its core.

Each design in this book tells its own unique story, showcasing a vision and the inspiration behind it. Many are driven by functionality and others by a natural instinct for fun. Whatever the vision, each design shares the common goal of giving back to the pets that inspired them.

Remember, design isn't only for humans but for our pets too. Whether you're a DIY enthusiast looking for a little inspiration, or maybe you're curious about how to update your pet's furnishings with a little style, barkitecture—just like architecture—is here to remind all of us that good design matters . . . no matter how many legs you have.

↑ Is it a panda? Or is it a dog? Marley's costume at the 2022 Triangle Barkitecture event goes great with the PawRabola designed by Duda|Paine Architects, PA (page 98).

→ This floppy-eared pup is happy to welcome you to Triangle Barkitecture from the PAUSE & PAWS by OBA (page 41).

Furry Furnishings

INTERIOR BARKITECTURE

Although a dog's ancestors may have spent their entire lives out in the wild and sleeping on the ground, a more sophisticated age calls for a more thoughtful approach to how we design and organize our living spaces so that they include a spot for our furry friends.

Gone are the days when our pups lacked dedicated spaces for their midday snoozies, cozy nooks close to their humans, or stylized storage for their toys and treats. In this chapter, we explore the innovative world of interior barkitecture, where the needs of our pups are seamlessly integrated into the design and aesthetics of our homes.

Barkitects are more than prepared to handle the challenge of crafting designs that blend style with functionality. Whether it's modern furniture pieces that complement your home's aesthetic or bold showpieces destined to become the focal point of any room, these designs rethink the way we live with our pets. Who says that being pet-friendly can't also be chic?

THE NUT HOUSE

A true love letter to the city it was made in—Raleigh, North Carolina—affectionately known as the City of Oaks. The Nut House by Redline Design combines both the charm of the city's identity and expert-level craftsmanship and woodworking. The unique pet retreat pays tribute to Raleigh's iconic acorn symbol, with its acorn shape and cleverly designed cap that can be removed to reveal a hidden storage compartment. But the real star of the show may be the ultra-cozy, plush interior that invites any pet to curl up and enjoy their midafternoon naps in style. The blend of natural materials and precision in the design make The Nut House not only functional but also a barkitecture masterpiece that bridges design aesthetic and pet comfort.

← Just look at how happy Bonbon is in The Nut House—as happy as a squirrel with an . . . acorn. And no matter how many acorns he may eat, there's plenty of room for growth in this house.

↑ The Nut House won the red ribbon for Best in Show at the 2023 Triangle Barkitecture.

BLUEPRINT

Off the drawing board and into your home, the Blueprint by Integrated Design and Lynch Mykins is engineered to entertain your pet with style and innovation. Your pup will love cozying up in the Blueprint's nook, where interactive puzzle walls—including the much-loved tennis-ball wall—offer endless amusement. Humans can even get in on some of the fun playing tennis-ball pickup once your pup is done taking them all out! This modular design isn't just striking, it's practical too, and can be easily dismantled to store in its custom box when playtime's over.

↑ Archie is a sweet senior rescue pup from Hope Animal Rescue. He was kind enough to take a break from the tennis-ball wall and pose for a cute picture. Now that he has your attention, this old man does love to be held and get scratches.

ULTIMUTT HUT

The Ultimutt Hut by Studio 310 offers a modern, cozy retreat for your pet while doubling as an elegant piece of interior barkitecture. Built with vertically stacked plywood ribs, this modular cube creates a visually striking design that allows your pet to lounge comfortably within a voided-out nook.

With clean lines and minimalist structure, it makes a perfect end table or accent piece in a contemporary home. Dark side panels both complement and provide contrast to the natural wood finish, while a brightly colored cushion adds a vibrant touch to the sleek design. The Ultimutt Hut is more than just a pet bed; it's a functional, stylish addition that enhances your home's aesthetic while giving your pet a relaxing, cushioned space.

↑ Little Michelle Myers is from a Halloween-themed litter of puppies rescued by Freedom Ride Rescue. But don't worry—this little pup is only here to kill you with cuteness.

← The Ultimutt Hut is made with contrasting colors for that modern yet minimal look.

HYGGE

Inspired by the Danish concept of "hygge" (pronounced *hue-gah*), which embodies warmth, coziness, and comfort, Hygge by LS3P and Lynch Mykins brings that same atmosphere to your pet's space. This elegant barkitecture design features gentle curves that cradle your pet, creating a cozy, secure environment. The interlocking wooden pieces allow for flexible configurations, adjusting the space to suit your needs by sliding the different sizes in and out. Depending on how you adjust it, underneath the table can be a smaller nook for your cat, a larger area for a bigger dog to lounge in, or even simply storage.

↓ Posed on top of the table (instead of underneath) is Firefly from Hope Animal Rescue.

→ To complement the cozy dog space below, Hygge also includes a matching wall installation for cats. Crafted from the same curved wood, the shelves offer the perfect playground for cats to explore, or you can use them for storage or displays.

HYGGE

ACRYLICK

Acrylick by Cline Design Associates combines straightforward assembly with pet-friendly function, giving even the most prominent Swedish furniture makers a run for their money. This modular structure uses interlocking wood supports and sleek acrylic panels that form a translucent roof—offering shade as well as plenty of natural light for your pup.

This build also comes with the ease of interchangeable opaque panels when more shade is desired. The panels can be extended to create an overhang on one end while leaving the other open for ventilation. Each piece is precision-cut with bone-shaped slots for easy assembly, adding both a playful touch and a quick setup for travel or storage.

↑ **For that dog who wants to spend most of their time outside, Acrylick is the perfect barkitecture for sunbathing.**

PAWDENZA

The Pawdenza by Hanbury with Brasfield & Gorrie and Unrefined Designs takes modern furniture design to the next level with its sleek versatility that adds a stylish pet nook to any home. This unique credenza doubles as both a sophisticated storage solution and a cozy retreat for your pet. The drop-down bed folds away quickly and easily, creating a gorgeous, contoured wood surface that turns heads even when closed. Inside, a concealed storage space is provided for toys and treats, keeping everything organized and close at hand. Whether in use or tucked away neatly, this piece combines beauty and functionality, making it perfect for pet lovers who value style as much as comfort.

↑ Santanna wants you to know that this drop-down bed is the best surprise retreat in the house. This sweet pup was found abandoned and in pretty rough shape, but thanks to Friends of Wake County Animal Center, he's now a part-time barkitecture model.

PAWS

This easy-to-assemble, modular barkitecture design by the CPL team was inspired by Puppies Actively Wishing for Shelter (PAWS). It was a standout for interior barkitecture standards at the 2019 Triangle Barkitecture competition with its stylish storage and, of course, one of the comfiest seats in the house for your pup. Sure to be an attention-grabbing addition to your home, PAWS ensures your pet always has a stylish space by your side.

→ **There is no shortage of storage and surface area for PAWS. Store an extra blanket on top, treats and plants on one side, and food and water bowls on the other.**

BARKSIDE TABLE

What's better than one extremely stylized and expertly crafted end table for your home? How about three different tables that neatly nest inside of each other when not in use? The Barkside Table by IA Interior Architects ensures that your pet has a nice resting spot they can grow into, plus room for two of their furry friends.

→ **This pup seems to have found the right-size home for your home, while also serving as the perfect model for this compact and functional end table.**

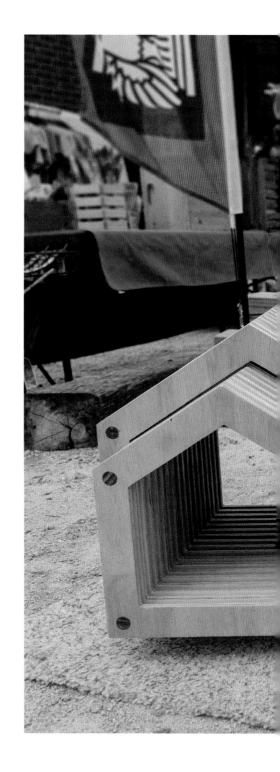

BUDDY BLOCK

If you're a fan of retro brain teasers, you'll love the playful inspiration behind Buddy Block by Szostak Design and Szostak Build. Drawing from the classic Rubik's Cube, this barkitecture is more than just easy on the eyes; it's cleverly crafted, cubic sanctuary for your pet. Made with a natural wood finish and those beautifully mitered corners, Buddy Block transforms a simple geometric concept into a functional and stylish lounging spot for your furry friend.

While we love the cube, the playful gaps encourage a bit of mischievous fun. We can already imagine a cat hiding inside, paws sneaking through the openings, to surprise anyone who dares walk by! Whether it's for play or relaxation, Buddy Block brings a modern, nostalgic twist to your home décor.

BARC

When we say this barkitecture rocks, we mean it in both the design and literal sense. With its elegantly curved wooden structure, the bARC by kasper architects + associates incorporates a gentle rocking motion into your pup's new favorite lounge spot, offering both relaxation and style. Perfectly engineered with two structural wood ribs, this barkitecture allows for a subtle sway that's sure to lull your pet into a restful state.

Between the ribs, recycled wood slats create a sturdy yet sustainable base for an ultra-comfy bed. Meanwhile, the top seamlessly curves upward to hold a sewn fabric canopy, offering your pup a shady retreat. Whether indoors or outdoors, bARC ensures your pet stays cool, comfy, and totally relaxed.

→ Sorry, but you're going to need to find another seat. Aeries the Samoyed floof wants to make sure the durability of this rocker is solid. (It is, he just doesn't want to move.)

← "If I fits, I sits" is always the motto we abide by in barkitecture, and this pup has found the perfect-size hangout in this house that's shaped like a game.

BUILD A BARK

This barkitecture creation offers both beauty and functionality and can be packed flat for easy storage and transportation. Build A Bark by Studio 310 allows you to quickly rearrange your interior layout or take your pet's setup on the go without any fuss. Whether you're opting for a semipermanent indoor lounge or a quick outdoor retreat, this design makes sure your pet's space is as convenient as it is visually striking.

Constructed primarily from plywood, the build includes a built-in food and water station and features a coated floor that simplifies cleanup. The bed can also be tailored to match your home's aesthetic, ensuring it blends seamlessly into any room.

→ **Build A Bark offers a functional design with interchangeable mats for the times when your dog wants to sit in the sun or shade.**

HEXAPAWD

Inspired by your dog's favorite six-sided shape, the HexaPawd by LS3P and Lynch Mykins is a versatile indoor or outdoor retreat with a geometrically appealing design that's also comfy and cozy for your pet. The sturdy hexagonal wood ribs form an open yet protective structure, giving your pet a dedicated shaded spot to unwind. With an integrated foldout bench between the ribs, this build allows you to join your pet for a moment of relaxation and bonding. When not in use, the bench seamlessly folds back into the frame. This pet-friendly hideaway truly combines comfort and flexibility with a modern twist.

↓ When you find the perfect size barkitecture you just have to get a picture. This distinguished gentleman looks like he knows good design when he sees it.

→ The unique shape of the HexaPawd allows multiple dogs to enjoy a spot of their own. For families with more than two furry friends, this barkitecture might just be for you. There's even a place for you to sit on the foldout bench.

BARKITECTURE

For the pet parent who loves to entertain, the BARkitecture by REdesign.build and REarchitecture serves up a fun and functional barkitecture that doubles as a bar cart. Whether you're mixing up another Paw-loma or a classic Frenchie 75, this build will make sure your pup has a spot to hang out and still be the center of attention as they deserve. The beautiful wood finish gives way to a comfy built-in alcove for your pet while the rest of the cart provides plenty of storage for your glassware and chilled bottles (or more dog treats), with a marble top perfect for serving up your creations and impressing your guests.

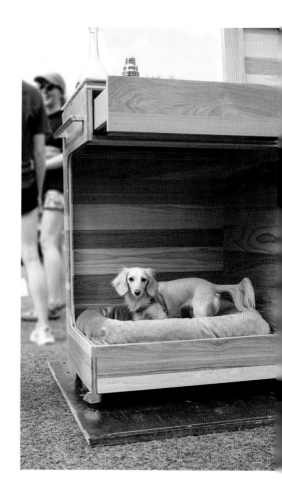

→ **This pup is ready to unwind in a cozy spot he found in the BARkitecture, where comfort always meets cocktail hour.**

PAUSE & PAWS

The PAUSE & PAWS by O'Brien Atkins Associates is a sleek, modern bench designed to do more than just look good; it's also crafted to strengthen the bond between you and your pup. Whether it's one continuous bench or two separate chairs, this versatile piece ensures your furry friend can relax by your side in comfort. The beautiful wood ribs and slats showcase expert

↑ **This playful pup knows just the right spot to sit and relax—even saving a spot for you to join them. Please provide a few scratches to say thanks!**

craftsmanship, while the pop of bright orange adds a playful yet practical touch to your pup's lounging area. Offering an easy-to-clean space, this thoughtfully sized and designed barkitecture is the perfect seating solution for shared and meaningful downtime.

THE BARKER AT
THE PURRSERVE

Your pets will love checking in to the The Barker at the Purrserve by Planworx Architecture! This multilevel space is designed for pet-loving households with both cats and dogs. It offers cozy ground-level and elevated spaces that cater to each pet's unique lounging style. Built with sustainability in mind, the structure incorporates reclaimed materials, including architectural samples, giving it an eco-friendly edge. Thoughtful window placements and overhangs also add to the design's appeal, offering pets comfortable lookouts from the comfort of their home. It's a stylish sanctuary that marries sustainable design with pet comfort.

↓ With cozy spots for all sizes, we're sure your pup will find the best room at The Barker. They may have to share the upper levels with your cat, but this little adoptable from Hope Animal Rescue says he doesn't mind.

→ Taking doghouse and making it dog hotel, Planworx created this multilevel cozy pad so that small pups can hang out together.

PAWFEE TABLE

The Pawfee Table by Clark Nexsen seamlessly combines modern elegance with pet-friendly features, creating a multifunctional centerpiece for your living room. The striking wood frame adds a warm, sophisticated touch, while its angular lines bring a stylish modern aesthetic to any room. Beneath the beautiful, functional wood tabletop lies a cozy nook where your furry friend can relax within reach, making it their new favorite hideaway. The design even incorporates some open shelving for keeping essentials close at hand while maintaining a sleek look. Whether you're entertaining or just unwinding with your favorite show, the Pawfee Table makes sure your pup has the best (and comfiest) seat in the house.

↓ **A perfect fit for the perfect floof! This cozy nook created by the Pawfee Table's angular design is approved by Astro for both style and comfort.**

ROCK'N DOG

For the music lover and their discerning pup, the Rock'n Dog by Knock on Wood by Enrique is a tune-loving doghouse. With its sleek and stylish frame drawing inspiration from the classic triangle-shaped roof of a traditional doghouse, the design is updated with modern elements to suit your pet's comfort and add a stylish piece of furniture in your home.

But it's not just about looks; this build is all about creating a welcoming space that's perfect for the musically inclined pet parent. The center of the design features a plush, built-in dog bed, giving your pup a comfortable nook to relax in while you spin tunes. Up top, find a spot for your record player and storage for your favorite vinyl, making it ideal to showcase your good taste in music. Your furry friend surely won't use this as a spot to lie around and judge your dance moves.

↑ Simba was his owner's muse in the creation of the Rock'n Dog, and it's obvious when you see this handsome boy fit so perfectly in the space. Simba is happy with whatever music his owner has spinning, as long as he has a comfy spot like this by their side.

STEP PAW-SITIN

Thoughtfully crafted and beautifully designed, the Step Paw-Sitin by Clark Nexsen and Raleigh Reclaimed brings both elegance and pup accessibility to your bedroom space. This expertly built piece sits gracefully at the foot of the bed with a rich wood finish and a padded top for added comfort where you or your pet can rest when it's not time for bedtime. The pullout steps are a clever touch, locking securely into place to ensure stability, while easily sliding back into a streamlined profile when not in use. For those nights when your pet prefers their own space, there's even a cozy built-in bed that gives them a perfect spot to curl up just in case you're snoring a bit too loud.

→ Watch and learn. Once the steps are pulled out and locked in, all one needs to do is step one paw at a time and then sit! Now you're Step Paw-Sitin!

BARKSIDE BUNGALOW

Inspired by mid-century modern fireplace designs, the Barkside Bungalow by Gensler and Oak City Customs is a cozy, stylish retreat for your pup.

Stacked plywood forms the structure to create a distinctive void for lounging and evoke the warmth of a fireplace aesthetic while delivering pet comfort. The thoughtful design includes a removable top, perfect for convenient toy or treat storage that you can grab and go for your next adventure. Whether it's a functional piece in your living room or a stylish pet nook, this bungalow brings multifunctionality and mid-century charm to your space.

← **Don't worry; this fireplace isn't cooking up anything except a stinking cute dog.**

TANGLED TAILS HOUSE

The Tangled Tails House by HDR is designed with sleek angles that carve out the perfect space in your home for a doghouse. This innovative barkitecture provides a cozy retreat for a playful pup or curious cat and serves as a display shelf for you. Its sharp, modern silhouette includes a built-in toy pouch for easy access to pet essentials, blending practical function with architectural appeal. Perfect for pets who love to stay close, the Tangled Tails House keeps toys, treats, and comfort within paw's reach. This doghouse is ideal for homes where pet-friendly style is a priority.

→ **Shaded bed? Check. Toys? Check. One happy pup? Check! The Tangled Tails House makes for a happy pet when you've got all your pet's comforts in one place.**

← Doesn't this dog look dapper inside the North Carolina Museum of Bark by BSA LifeStructures (page 67)?

Barks and Recreation

EXTERIOR BARKITECTURE

The call of the outdoors is sometimes just too strong—whether it's the allure of a squirrel, the need to patrol the yard, or simply answering nature's call. In Barks and Recreation, we explore how barkitects have reimagined outdoor play and activities, crafting spaces where pets can embrace their wild side while keeping a careful eye on their humans.

Gone are the days of standard prefab doghouses with gabled roofs or plastic igloos. Instead, this chapter highlights innovative designs that provide your pet with everything they need for outdoor adventures—like offering shade and cooling during hot summer days, or interactive play spaces that turn the backyard into a dog's paradise.

These builds marry functionality with fun, transforming outdoor spaces into extensions of your pet's home. From eco-friendly materials to thoughtful layouts, the following barkitecture showcases the art of creating an outdoor environment that's as engaging for your pet as it is stylish for your home.

THAT'S SO FETCH

Talk about an eye-catching design. That's So Fetch by Cline Design Associates makes a bold statement with its foldable design and pop of blue among the warm wood tones. The design pays homage to a more traditional doghouse form, but the foldable panels at the roof allow the structure to expand and open an upper level for pups to explore. On the lower level, your pup can find plenty of room to cuddle up while the upper level gives them a better view.

Of course, we cannot forget about the tempting wall of tennis-ball storage specially designed to make sure a game of fetch is never too far away. Watch your pup make a quick getaway using the movable partition in the back that makes this such a clever and exciting build.

← We're just grateful that Hiccup took a moment away from playing with all the tennis balls to take a cute picture and show off this pawsome barkitecture. This rescue pup from Hope Animal Rescue could not get enough of this build!

PAWVILION

Inspired by Raleigh's iconic Catalano House, the Pawvilion by Gensler and SEAS is a mid-century modern retreat for your pet. The design features a stunning hyperbolic paraboloid roof (sometimes lovingly referred to as the "potato chip"), which casts plenty of shade for the ultra-comfy bed below. This cozy yet open setup lets your pup rest securely while embracing the architectural flair of the structure. The clean white frame paired with a bright orange bed creates a striking and stylish tribute, bringing Eduardo Catalano's innovative spirit to a functional design for your furry friend.

↑ Benjamin Barker from Freedom Ride Rescue found a cozy spot to rest at the 2023 Triangle Barkitecture event. And in even greater news, he also found his forever home shortly after the event!

→ Just imagine this bright white structure in your backyard. Your dog will have the coolest house on the block.

RETRO ROVER RETREAT

The Retro Rover Retreat is a tribute to mid-century modern architecture, blending sleek simplicity with playful design elements to create the ultimate hangout for your pup. With its shallow roofline and clean geometric form, this doghouse evokes the timeless elegance of mid-century design while ensuring your pet feels right at home.

In true mid-century modern fashion, the Retro Rover Retreat features a fun twist with the acrylic accent wall, designed as a safe space to store tennis balls. This adds a pop of playful sophistication, but also a temptation-filled display that is sure to catch a dog's attention.

← **Puck from Triangle Beagle Rescue may be small now, but he wants you to know that he'll grow up to fit perfectly in the Retro Rover Retreat and play with every tennis ball in it!**

THE WOOF WAGON

The Woof Wagon is specially designed with veterans and their service dogs in mind, offering a versatile, cozy space to keep a vet's best friend comfortable, both indoors and outdoors. The thoughtfully designed canopy provides much-needed shade and shelter, while a soft, snug bed ensures your K9 companion can rest easy no matter where the journey leads.

Designed by service-disabled veteran-owned businesses Apogee Consulting Group and BZ Construction, this barkitecture entry rolls onto the stage not only to raise awareness for pet rescues but also to highlight the needs of veterans and their service dogs. The Woof Wagon embodies both function and care, ensuring that these incredible dogs have a comfortable place to rest while continuing their essential work by their owners' sides.

← **Jaqweenie has his bow tie on and is ready to vet the special dog who gets to hitch a ride in their new home.**

CAMP
BARKITECTURE

HH Architecture may call this design
Camp Barkitecture, but rest assured,
your pup is about to be glamping in
style. Sleeping outside on the ground
is much too primitive for today's
sophisticated dogs, so this raised bed
makes sure they will be relaxed and
comfortable when enjoying the great
outdoors. The bright yellow tent with a
collapsible and flat pack design means
it won't be too much hassle to bring
on your next camping trip—just make
sure you have your own space because
your pup won't want to share. The white
shade is light enough to let in some light
while protecting from the elements,
and the comfy bed means your pup just
might skip that next hike to enjoy a little
more relaxation.

→ Living the glamping life, this pup
has snagged the comfiest spot at Camp
Barkitecture. We hope you brought your own
tent because this one's taken!

T.L.C.

Built with a thoughtful approach to play and bonding, the T.L.C. by HH Architecture is more than just a play structure; it's an all-encompassing outdoor retreat where pets and their owners can Train, Learn, and Connect. Designed for exercise and engagement, it offers climbing areas to challenge your pup and keep them active. The folding structure is equipped with clever storage solutions including foldable spaces for food and water bowls, which tuck away neatly when not in use. For those relaxing moments, there's a built-in bench where you can sit and enjoy downtime together while playtime is always within reach.

↑ Talk about top dog—this little guy has climbed to the top of T.L.C. and just may be looking for their reward . . . treat, please?

→ T.L.C. is an innovative mix of functionality and fun, making it easy for you and your pet to share outdoor moments together.

BOWHAUS

By channeling the clean lines, simple forms, and functional beauty of Bauhaus design, the BowHaus by HagerSmith Design is a minimalist outdoor retreat for your pup. Its removable turf base ensures comfort while grounding your pet in nature, and the open slatted-wood walls provide shelter and ventilation, allowing a breeze to flow through. String lights across the ceiling add a cozy, modernist touch to illuminate this build, day or night, with style that honors the famous "form follows function" philosophy.

↑ Suns out, tongues out! BowHaus is the perfect shady spot to grab a quick rest and to rehydrate before your next adventure.

← Like Bauhaus architecture, which focuses on harmony between a building's function and aesthetic, the BowHaus's geometric wood construction serves both design and practical needs.

PAWGODA

The PawGoda by RGG Architects + Bull City Designs is intended to be a calming sanctuary where dogs can find their inner Zen amid nature. The beautifully crafted wood base supports a metal frame shaped in a traditional pagoda style, inspired by the architectural elegance of East Asia. Fully open on all sides, the structure invites ample airflow and sunlight, making it a perfect structure to decorate with climbing plants and create a natural green canopy overhead. Along with the grass sections sharing the deck, your dog can truly be surrounded by nature when practicing their namasit and namastay.

↑ Don't let the name fool you—little Elvis here can't be rock 'n' roll all the time. Instead, he's looking to find a Zen moment with his new barkitecture!

→ With a nature-focused design, this build blends seamlessly into your garden and creates the perfect place for your pup to relax and enjoy the fresh air.

PETSHELL

The PetShell by Arco Design/Build provides a thoughtfully crafted outdoor retreat for your dog, designed with cost-effective materials that balance comfort, durability, and minimal waste. With a base structure of precisely cut plywood sheets, the PetShell optimizes its material use while a spray-on concrete texture adds a unique contrast and enhances durability. The lookout deck on top has removable turf for easy cleaning or space for a comfortable bed where your dog can squirrel watch in your backyard. This barkitecture also offers your pup a shady, enclosed space underneath for restful naps.

↑ Whether a pup needs shelter from the elements or just a comfortable place to lie down, this barkitecture has it all.

NORTH CAROLINA MUSEUM OF BARK

This pup-tastic design by BSA LifeStructures brings the art world to your dog's doorstep! Inspired by the iconic architecture of Raleigh's North Carolina Museum of Art, the build incorporates elements of the museum's park, with its three sculptured rings and the sleek rectangular gallery famous for its beautifully diffused light. The design also features panels like the museum's striking aluminum rain screens, giving a shimmering backdrop that resembles the environment.

Whether your dog is lounging in the sun or wandering around, they'll feel right at home—and maybe they'll even be inspired to become the next great canine artist. Who knows? With a home like this, your pup might just be the next Paw-casso!

→ **Peony from Change of Heart Pit Bull Rescue may only have three legs, but that doesn't take away the pep in her step. This doghouse looks like an extravagant exhibit piece and makes every dog feel like one too.**

PUP PAWD

The Pup Pawd by kasper architects + associates is the ultimate cozy hideaway for your pet, featuring a removable top section made from lightweight acoustic panels crafted from recycled content. When the top is removed, the structure showcases your pet's stylish space and also adds some more airflow on those breezy days. However, the acoustic shell may come in handy while your pup snoozes and snores in this pod.

Incorporating biophilic design (nature-inspired design elements), the Pup Pawd brings a touch of nature to your home, blending function with natural aesthetics. The sturdy base also doubles as a convenient storage compartment, perfect for stashing your dog's toys or gardening supplies for trimming those green walls!

→ Taking a well-deserved break, this pup has found a nice shady spot to rest in the Pup Pawd while posing in the green-inspired design.

← With a hexagonal base, there's plenty of space for your dog, and their friends, to enjoy this barkitecture!

RUFFWAVE

Catch a wave and some shade with the RuffWave by RGG Architects and Bull City Designs. Inspired by the cresting wave every surfer dreams of, this barkitecture creation lets your pup hang ten in style. The sturdy metal frame gives the structure a unique look while the richly colored wood decking adds warmth and contrast. This stylish setup is sure to make your pup the top dog on the boardwalk while giving those beach bum vibes.

↓ Rough waves are no problem for this little Frenchie. Just look at those sharp wings! Fearlessness and a sturdy structure mix perfectly for the best barkitecture models.

← Perfect for any surfer dog at heart, give your dog a house that matches its vibe. Don't forget some beach-themed toys to pull the scene together.

POOCH PORCH

The Pooch Porch by Clark Nexsen is a modern interpretation of a traditional front porch, thoughtfully crafted for our loyal furry friends. This design uses a series of intricately routed wood frames, joined with dowel construction, to support a large translucent roof that allows soft, diffused light to filter through while shielding pups from harsh sunrays. Your pooch will love lounging on the cozy, removable bed while watching the world go by, just like they would on a classic porch. With an added planter built into the frame, the Pooch Porch also brings a touch of greenery to any space.

↑ Attention comes easy when you're as cute as Jaqweenie. We're still not sure if he's ever found a piece of barkitecture that he didn't like. In fact, we're fairly sure he thinks the competition is for him, and we're OK with that.

← If anybody deserves a cozy porch to lounge on, next to the flowers, it's our furry friends who wait patiently for their owners to come home.

→ This prancing pup is so excited to see everyone at the 2024 Triangle Barkitecture near the Lincoln Dogs (page 89) build.

Greenest Paws

SUSTAINABLE BARKITECTURE

As our world becomes more aware of the impact of design on the environment, it's no surprise that barkitecture has embraced sustainability with open paws. For the eco-conscious pet owner, creating a home for your furry companion isn't just about aesthetics; it's about ensuring the materials, energy use, and design are just as thoughtful as the rest of your home.

In this chapter, we showcase the Greenest Paws in barkitecture, where pet design meets sustainability. These pet homes are often constructed with renewable materials and feature energy-saving technologies like solar panels, all while designed with nature in mind. From upcycled materials to eco-friendly design solutions, each build focuses on reducing waste while maximizing comfort.

These sustainable designs prove that barkitecture can be both stylish and earth friendly. With the goal of creating spaces that benefit both pets and our planet, these builds inspire us to think beyond the traditional and reimagine what green living looks like—for both our pets and us.

So, whether your pup is lounging in a solar-powered doghouse or snoozing in a structure made from repurposed wood, these designs ensure that both your pet and the planet are well taken care of. After all, who says pets can't have a paw-sitive impact on our environment?

BOWWOW HOUSE

A true testament to the power of upcycling, the BowWow House by RND Architects, PA takes a forgotten piece of retired furniture and transforms it into a stylish, mid-century modern–inspired statement piece for both your living room and your pup. The original furniture is carefully refinished and opens up to create a cozy, inviting space where your pet can relax in comfort.

This revamped design features an elevated food and water station for convenience and a bold pop of color that beautifully complements the rich wood tones. The additional accent panel not only adds visual interest but also gives your pet a bit more privacy while repurposing the original design elements to merge function and sustainable elegance.

↑ A long day of checking out amazing barkitecture can be just a little too exhausting, as we can see with little Babushka Anya taking a quick snooze in the comfiest spot she could find.

← This barkitecture uses a mix of striking patterns and bold colors to create a conversation piece in any house.

THE MUTT HUTT

The Mutt Hutt by Moseley Architects is your pup's personal relaxation station, especially after a long day working "like a dog." What pup would not want to go for a mar-grrr-rita in this cabana-inspired design? The floor uses a reclaimed wood pallet as a base for the highly sustainable and locally sourced bamboo stalks that make up the walls and support the straw roof. The design goes the extra step for sustainability while leaning into the tropical vibes, incorporating solar-powered tiki lights so your pet can keep the party going into the night. It's five o'clock somewhere and The Mutt Hutt ensures that your pet is always ready for a good time.

↓ If there is one pup who knows how to appreciate taking it easy with a little pamper sesh, it would be Jaqweenie. This rescue pup is a local celebrity known for being a little dramatic, but when you look this cute, there really are no limits to what you can get away with. If the bar is out of cosmo-paw-litans, he'll gladly accept a pup cup instead.

→ The Mutt Hutt is crafted with a wooden sideboard for refreshments and a bright sea urchin–shaped bed for lounging.

OAK PAWVILION

The Oak Pawvilion by kasper architects + associates is the new backyard go-to spot—a sustainable outdoor retreat for your pup to relax and perhaps even try out their green paw. Upcycled wood pallets make up most of the structure, providing shelter—they are spaced apart enough for a nice cool breeze to pass through. Other materials include corrugated metal panels atop opaque plastic panels for some diffuse lighting—both rescued from an architectural-sample graveyard and put to good use. The Oak Pawvilion even includes your pup's own raised garden planter, perfect for small plantings.

→ Admiring your barkitecture's new succulent garden is one thing, but we have a sneaking suspicion that this pup wouldn't mind if this were converted into a treat station.

WHOLE-LEASH IT

Nothing says "I love dogs" like a piece of furniture made from color-coordinated dog accessories! The Whole-Leash It by Hanbury is a modern, stylish design that creatively reuses old dog leashes to form a functional piece for you and your pup. Supported by a wooden frame, this unique furniture item is a nod to the wear and tear of every pet parent's journey. The leashes not only add color and texture but also bring a fun, upcycled element to your home. While your pet rests underneath, there's a seat on top for you too. The Whole-Leash It is a cozy spot for both of you to unwind after a walk—or to inspire you for the next one.

↓ Soda wants you to know that he's a world-class snuggler. If you just take a seat in this barkitecture, he's ready to prove it!

SUMMER PAW COOL

When the summer heat is relentless, the Summer Paw Cool by Coffman Engineers is the perfect oasis to ensure your pup stays cool while enjoying time outside with you. Designed with sustainability and comfort in mind, this barkitecture combines innovative eco-friendly features to create the ultimate chill-out zone for your pet.

Solar panels power the structure, providing energy for built-in lights and a fan that keeps air circulating to ensure

↑ With all that extra floof, a pup really starts to appreciate barkitectures that offer a shady spot and a splash zone to hang out in.

your dog stays comfortable even during the hottest days of the year. But that's not all—the Summer Paw Cool also includes a rainwater harvesting system that fills a built-in pool, giving your pup a refreshing spot to splash around and cool off. Made from reclaimed wood and pallets, the structure not only looks good but also is environmentally conscious.

PAWPRAIRIE BENCH

The PawPrairie Bench by Tara Girolimon is a sustainable, nature-infused escape for you and your pet, crafted with a unique blend of repurposed pet crates. With the reuse of these crates, the design establishes a resilient foundation that holds a sturdy bench, inviting you to share outdoor moments with your furry friend. Each side is reinforced with tightly pressed wood panels, transforming them into surfaces ideal for nurturing moss or plants, or even forming gabions for a unique, natural aesthetic in your landscape. Inside, the crates remain fully usable, providing convenient storage for toys or essentials, or even an extra sheltered nook where your pet can relax and unwind.

→ **These living walls not only add a calming green element to the structure but also allow the design to blend beautifully into its outdoor surroundings.**

DOG-TON ARENA

A love letter to Raleigh's iconic Dorton Arena, DOG-TON ARENA by IA Interior Architects turns your pet into the star of the show. This creative barkitecture not only captures the spirit of a historic local landmark but also incorporates renewable energy to keep your pet's stage cool and comfortable. The spacious "stage" is designed to hold your pet's favorite bed for maximum comfort, with additional built-in storage, feeding stations for convenience, and a playful planter in the back to add a touch of nature.

↑ The unique roof features photovoltaic panels that power an energy-efficient fan to keep your pup cool during hot summer days.

← This one is for the pup who was born to be in the spotlight and have the grandest stage set just for them.

↑ Bernie may only be a pup, but he knows good design when he sees it. This little one could barely contain the tail wags in his first barkitecture experience.

← This dog is here to convince you any pooch can fit in this house. Trust him! There's even a back window!

LINCOLN DOGS

We're honestly not sure who is going to fight over this more—your pup or your kids! Lincoln Dogs by Cline Design Associates is a life-size take on the classic children's toy and early childhood architect experience, Lincoln Logs! It's fully customizable to fit dogs of any shape or size, transforming it into a couple of Chihuahua bungalows or one Bernese mountain dog cabin.

What truly makes this design special is that it is not made of logs but recycled cardboard tubes collected from rolls of every architect's favorite paper size of 30 by 42 inches (76 by 107 cm). This design ensures that these tubes won't go to waste and are instead notched to fit together perfectly to build the doghouse of your pup's dreams.

← **This cool cat invites you to embrace the vibes of Woofstock (page 95) at the 2022 Triangle Barkitecture.**

Pawsitively Unconventional

UNIQUE BARKITECTURE

Barkitecture celebrates more than just stylish and functional designs—creativity is welcomed to run off leash to where the unexpected takes center stage. In Pawsitively Unconventional, the boundaries of pet architecture are pushed to new heights, proving that there's no one right way to design a home for our four-legged friends.

This chapter highlights the bold, imaginative, and delightfully unconventional. Here, you'll find designs that redefine what is possible: from spots for a pup on the move to modular structures that can be reconfigured to function in different ways. These builds are more than just pet homes; they're expressions of the barkitects' artistic visions and inventive problem-solving we've come to expect.

Whether it's a gravity-defying design, a house that doubles as a moving adventure, or a structure that can transform and adapt, the creations in this chapter challenge everything you thought you knew about barkitecture. Expect the unexpected, because for a barkitect the only limit is imagination.

91

FURIGAMI

We're not sure what is the pet equivalent of a Swiss Army knife, but the Furigami by IA Interior Architects may be the closest thing. This transformational barkitecture design is built for flexibility, with multiple configurations that adapt to the needs of your busy pet.

Whether serving as a stylish end table with a cozy pet nook, folding out into a room divider, or transforming into a treat play maze, the Furigami delivers versatility in every fold. Its beautiful wood aesthetic and expert craftsmanship ensure it's not just functional but also a statement piece that blends seamlessly into your home's design.

↑ Even when there isn't a lot of space, the Furigami is designed just right for pups who love a snug spot by your side.

← Here is the Furigami folded into a doghouse and end table.

WOOFSTOCK

If you're looking for a groovy spot for your pet, look no further than the Woofstock by Planworx Architects. This whimsical design captures the free-spirited essence of the Woodstock festival, where love, peace, and pets coexist in harmony. The majority of the base and tent structure is made up of upcycled wood pallets that can be collapsed for easy portability—perfect for those impromptu outdoor jam sessions. Secondhand fabrics were used to create the tent, backdrops, and bedding, making this a sustainable build that any flower child or pup will love.

↓ Groovy vibes only for this barkitecture this pup is living the dream at Woofstock where comfort and peace reign supreme.

← This cozy build comes with the fluffiest bed, concealed string lights, and, of course, a basket of toys for an optimal play area for your pet.

THE TRANSFORMATION STATION

For pet owners who value adaptability, The Transformation Station by Summit Design and Engineering Services offers the ultimate flexible pet accommodation. This barkitecture piece is equipped with foldable and pull-out compartments, allowing it to transform to suit your pet's mood—such as a cozy enclosed nook or an open, inviting space perfect for basking in the sun or stretching out. Whether your dog wants a private hideaway or an outdoor sundeck, this piece adapts to fit their preference. Additionally, hidden storage and built-in hooks keep all pet accessories in one convenient place, making it as organized as it is versatile.

← When this build opens up, the versatility starts to shine! Hang up your leashes, store your toys, and lay out some blankets. You'll never have to leave this doghouse anytime soon!

PAWRABOLA

Pups love a good Frisbee, and that was the starting inspiration for the PawRabola team at Duda|Paine Architects, PA. Combining playful design with modernist architectural influence, this piece of barkitecture makes a striking addition to any pet-friendly space.

A waffle-lattice wood structure forms the base, supporting a bold parabolic shell overhead made of Frisbee-like pieces. This unique canopy not only catches the eye but provides essential shade, ensuring your pup stays cool as they lounge in style—waiting for their next game of fetch. Modern, functional, and fun, PawRabola is as iconic as it is practical.

→ Granola is all smiles thanks to Freedom Ride Rescue. Once found wounded and abandoned, this resilient pup has made a remarkable recovery. He might even be dreaming up a beach trip after spending time under the hue of these blue disks.

WAGON TAILS

Your pet is about to live the ultimate glamping lifestyle with the Wagon Tails by Kilian Engineering. This pup-size camper comes equipped with all the amenities a spoiled pet could dream of, including a solar-powered fan for cooling on those extra warm days and remote-controlled lights to scare away all that goes bump in the night.

↓ **Every dog deserves to sleep in a camper and get that true camping experience. There's nothing like visiting the wonders of nature while having a comfortable bed to sleep in at night.**

THE FURBONACCI TABLE

↑ **The key word for this barkitecture is "functional." Turn your coffee table into a doghouse with The Furbonacci Table.**

The Furbonacci Table by Planworx Architecture provides a stylish coffee table and cozy hideaway for your pup or feline friend. Inspired by the Fibonacci sequence, the table's gently curving dowel rods support a butcher-block top, creating a unique look that's both artistic and sturdy. Along with a built-in resting spot, this piece features scratching posts to keep even your cat entertained. It's a beautiful blend of natural materials and playful design that ensures your pet has a space of their own—right at the center of your living space.

PUP SIDE-DOWN

The Pup Side-Down by BDHP is a versatile and eye-catching piece of interior barkitecture designed to make a statement and keep your living space flexible. Perfect for both you and your pets, this transformational design can be flipped upside down to reveal a whole new look and function, ensuring it never gets boring.

One configuration offers a cozy seating area for you to relax with a book—and, of course, a comfy space for your pup below. Flip it and it becomes either an elevated bed for your cat, a display shelf for you, or a cozy nook for your dog underneath. Whether you need a fresh aesthetic or just a different seating arrangement for your furry family, the Pup Side-Down has the flexibility to suit your mood and all of your pets' comfort needs!

↓ Comfort comes in different variations with the Pup Side-Down. When the tongue comes out, we think that means this pup is happy with the cushioned spot they've found—there's even some room left for you!

→ Upside down, right side up, flip it any way you want. This barkitecture gem is perfect for pups big or small, offering a comfy fit for every personality!

THE BARK ROYAL

Ahoy, Meow-ty! All aboard The Bark Royal by The Bobbitt Group, Inc. Although this vessel may not be exactly seaworthy, your pet will still dream of sailing the seven seas in their new pirate life—hook paw and eye patch not included. This barkitecture uses reclaimed wood for the base of the ship, featuring a bed below deck and a raised section to keep an eye on the horizon.

Not only can dogs enjoy this barkitecture, but your cat will have fun climbing the sails, trying to get to that annoying parrot resting atop the crow's nest. This barkitecture is ready to entertain both you and your pets!

↓ Setting sail for comfort and fun, this captain of The Bark Royal is ready for their next pawsome adventure on the high seas of your living room!

← Soda's shift is over and it's time for his nap, so you can find him below deck while someone else in the crew takes the wheel.

PAWTY FLIGHT

Designed for ultimate backyard summer cookouts is the Pawty Flight by The Bobbitt Group, Inc. This design flies high with its unique airplane structure that serves as a bar table for the adults. It also comes equipped with a couple tennis-ball launchers that make sure your best friend is being entertained and getting exercise while everyone else is enjoying the party. The base is conveniently designed to hold two party kegs, so the responsible thing to do would be to make sure one is a dog beer for your furry best friend. We hear that tennis-ball launchers are great entertainment for the kids and your "well-hydrated" friends too!

↑ This little beagle is posing inside the doggy aircraft, where there's a sweet little bed for him to rest on after chasing all those tennis balls. And if he had a few too many dog beers, talk about the convenience of putting a bed right next to the keg, am I right?

← The Pawty Flight is a stunning bright blue that just screams, "Let's have a good time!"

WHO LET THE KONG OUT!

What happens when your pup's favorite chew toy becomes larger than life? With Who Let the KONG Out! by The Bobbitt Group, Inc., your dog won't have to daydream any longer. Inspired by the iconically shaped KONG toy every chewer loves, this barkitecture design uses upcycled tires, transforming them into a massive, playful structure.

Coated in KONG's signature red hue, the recycled tires form a shady outdoor haven where your pet can finally relax and destroy their toys in peace. With the ultimate durability, this barkitecture has been rated "chew safe" for the strongest gnawers—a rarity these days in the world of design!

↑ Talk about a big upgrade! This foster from Triangle Beagle Rescue is living the life and enjoying the shade of this king-size KONG.

→ Who doesn't love KONG's classic chew toy? Especially when it's filled with treats or peanut butter—but in this case, it comes with a bed!

→ Bentley from Connie's Kittens is here to represent the Paws and Claws by LS3P and Clancy & Theys (page 125).

Meow-dern Purritecture

FELINE BARKITECTURE

Designing for dogs is one thing, but designing for cats? That's a whole new ball of yarn. In Meow-dern Purritecture, we showcase the same incredible creativity and craftsmanship of barkitecture, but with a feline twist. These builds are thoughtfully crafted nooks for lounging, perches for climbing, and playful spaces that cater to a cat's natural instincts for exploration, independence, and, of course, catnaps.

Creating the *purrfect* home for a cat comes with its own set of unique challenges. After all, you might pour your heart into designing a comfy, elegant hideaway, only to find that your cat prefers the box it came in just a little more. That's the beauty of these cat-focused designs; it's about understanding cats' unique personalities and creating spaces that not only look great but offer the purrfect balance of comfort and curiosity for even the most discerning feline.

In this chapter, you'll see imaginative structures that speak to the soul of the cat—whether it's an elaborate climbing station, a sun-drenched perch, or a hidden retreat where they can keep a close eye on their humans. Purritecture is where style meets function for both our cats and us.

PAWFFEE TABLE

A stunning display of woodworking excellence and modern design, the Pawffee Table by Szostak Design brings elegance to any living room while subtly adding a special nook for your cat. The geometric wood frame that forms the table's supports include secluded ramps, leading your cat to the perfect-size space to lounge and silently judge your TV-viewing habits. Topped with a beautiful wood surface, this piece thoughtfully caters to both humans and pets without it screaming, "I'm a cat house."

← **These stuffed felines are the purrfect models to show how multiple cats can enjoy this sleek and spacious purritecture.**

CATARITAVILLE

We know the reason why your cat will be "wasting away again," and it's thanks to all the cozy hammocks they'll find in Cataritaville by Veterinary Architecture Unleashed. This delightful multilevel wooden deck is designed with your feline's relaxation in mind, providing several snug spots to settle in. The design features bright blue tones set against warm wood, creating a charming tropical vibe that makes a striking addition to your home.

When your cat isn't lounging around eating wet food out of margarita glasses, they'll be using the scratching posts or swatting at that parrot's head between searches for their lost shaker of treats.

→ **As you can see with this full view of Cataritaville, your cat will certainly waste some time exploring every corner of this build.**

Wastin' away in Cataritaville

KATTENHUIS

The bold pop of pink in the Kattenhuis by Hanbury is impossible to miss. Whether your cat prefers the comfort of a cozy nook close to the ground or a luxurious plush bed for sunbathing, this modernist design has your pet covered.

The plywood structure provides the perfect spot for private biscuit-making, with a snug bed nestled in its lower compartment. Above, the design transitions into a corrugated cardboard structure, offering your cat an ideal place to indulge in some extra scratching. Both stylish and functional, the Kattenhuis is designed to meet all your cat's lounging, scratching, and sunbathing needs while giving your home a modern flair.

← **With natural wood tones contrasted by striking pink and yellow accents, this piece makes a vibrant statement in any cat owner's home.**

KITTY KUBBIES

Meet Kitty Kubbies, the ultimate modular cat house that brings together playful design and practical function. Created by RND Architects, PA and Davie Construction Co. and inspired by the shapes of *Tetris*, this design offers a unique and dynamic furniture solution that caters to both feline playfulness and human aesthetics. With lightweight frames and carefully engineered interlocking slats, each unit is designed to stand alone or come together in a variety of shapes, making it as versatile as it is stylish. Whether you arrange it as a stand-alone coffee table, an eye-catching bookshelf, or an interactive play tower, Kitty Kubbies brings endless possibilities to your living space and is sure to keep you and your cat entertained.

Crafted with your feline friend's needs in mind, there are spots for a hidden litter box and cozy napping nooks, while scratch pads and hammocks keep your cat engaged and entertained.

↑ Dakota from Connie's Kittens is having a blast exploring the high perches of Kitty Kubbies. With so many opportunities at their paws, the choice between playing or relaxing is a tough one.

→ The modular units are designed to adapt to any corner of your home so that you can maximize the functionality of your space while adding some fun architectural flair.

CAT FLAT

The Cat Flat by RGG Architects and Bull City Designs is a cat attention captivator with its multilevel hidey-holes and beautifully curved, carpeted roof—perfect for keeping a lookout while sharpening those claws.

What sets this design apart is its clever use of upcycled materials. With 3D-printed corner brackets and plywood waste from furniture production, this barkitecture combines sustainability and style. Discarded packaging materials were repurposed for the roof to add a unique touch and create a space where your cat can explore, lounge, and play in eco-conscious comfort.

↓ Look at all those tiers! Your cat will have a blast discovering their purrfect cozy spot.

THE CAT CREDENZA

Designed with the sophisticated feline in mind, this stylish piece created by IA Interior Architects offers more than just a place for your cat to nap, hide, or take care of business; it's also a beautiful addition to your living space.

Stylishly crafted from wood with a subtle, warm finish, the credenza showcases its craftsmanship through carefully accented joinery, creating a sleek and minimalist look. Incorporating some playful cat-themed details, multiple cat compartments provide cozy spaces with hidden entry points and a concealed litter-box area that lets them take care of business in private. For your cat's lounging pleasure, there is a lookout perch at the top, situated at just the right height to knock off any of those silly prized trinkets humans like to display.

↑ **Enjoying the space and comfort of The Cat Credenza, Tofu from Connie's Kittens greatly appreciates the height advantage this bed grants her.**

ROCKET CAT

Prepare for lift-off with the Rocket Cat, an out-of-this-world design by Davis Kane Architects that's sure to send your feline companion on imaginary planetary adventures—all from the comfort of your living room. With its vibrant colors and whimsical shapes, this design is not afraid to make a bold statement, perfectly reflecting the playful and curious nature of our cats.

Made with sustainability in mind, this build also features recycled materials, ensuring it's as eco-conscious as it is fun. Each level is equipped with a base made of carpet samples, offering the ideal surface for scratching. Whether your cat is preparing for launch, climbing to new heights, or just in the mood for a scratch, the Rocket Cat provides the perfect launchpad for adventure and comfort.

↓ Gimli from Connie's Kittens was asked if he's ready to captain this rocket ship. There's definitely a hint of a space explorer shining in those blue eyes, so buckle up!

← Built for (space) exploration, the Rocket Cat has multiple levels to satisfy your cat's climbing instincts, with each tier providing a new vantage point for stargazing—or more likely, frantically swatting at all the stars hanging from the structure.

PAWS AND CLAWS

Designed for increasingly popular multi-pet households, Paws and Claws by LS3P and Clancy & Theys is a harmonious solution that ensures both your dog and cat have their own spaces—without any of the rivalry.

For our canine companions, the bottom section boasts a large orthogonal base with cozy, well-padded nooks perfect for lounging. Dogs can relax while keeping an eye on the tennis-ball wall—smartly designed with movable acrylic panels that allow for spontaneous games of fetch.

On the top of the structure, the form takes a more organic turn that caters to the curious and agile nature of cats. Elevated climbing platforms and a custom cat hammock reward feline explorers with a stylish, comfy lookout. With height and optimal vantage points, the entire upper area encourages cats to climb and explore to their hearts' desire.

← **Humans, perk up your ears! Ferrari from Connie's Kittens has a secret about this build. There's clever storage built into the design. Find a few shelves and a pull-out seat that doubles as additional storage on the side of this build.**

PAWDULAR SHELVING

The Pawdular Shelving by Arcadis is a contemporary twist on the classic bookcase, made to embrace your cat's playful and adventurous spirit. With multiple levels crafted from gorgeous wood with contrasting shades, it provides plenty of options for climbing and perching, letting you share your space in style with your feline friend. If your cat doesn't get enough of this build from all that, it also features a gravity feeder, making mealtimes for your pet only a pull of the lever away. And who knows? There might be room at the bottom for your pup to curl up if your cat allows it, bringing together all your pets in one seamless design.

→ Perched up high in Pawdular Shelving, Gimli knows exactly which spot is his, so we guess you'll just have to find another spot for all your human trinkets.

↑ No need to worry about weight limits, each basket can be occupied at the same time. This is either equivalent to a sleepover or an amusement park ride, depending on the arrangement.

← With three different pods, your cat is sure to find the best spot no matter the combination—just like Everest here, who felt the middle pod was just right, while Bruno preferred the top pod for its superior vantage point.

CLAW HOUSE

Let's be honest, no cardboard box could ever compete with this level of feline fun. Constructed from a sturdy birch plywood base and frame, the Claw House by CRB incorporates three claw-friendly cardboard baskets that can be arranged in various ways.

For adventurous kitties, the towering, multi-pod arrangement offers endless opportunities for climbing, leaping, and surveying their home from up on high. More introverted cats can enjoy a single pod configuration for a calm, elevated perch—ideal for that all-important midday snooze. For added convenience, there are even washable pillow covers to ensure their napping spots stay fresh and comfy.

Built with playful adaptability in mind, this build offers both excitement and relaxation for up to three cats, making it an amazing addition to any cat-loving household.

TALL TAILS BOOKSHELF

The Tall Tails Bookshelf by Moseley Architects is the ultimate fusion of functional home design and playful purritecture. Not only does it offer your feline friend a fun-filled playground—complete with tunnels, beds, toys, and elevated hideaways to explore—but it also serves as a sleek storage solution that will blend right in with your home's aesthetic. No bookshelf is complete without a space to display some books (about cats) and other personal trinkets. Maybe just be careful where you place the fragile stuff! There's even a cozy nook at the bottom that might be claimed by your pup, although with cats, we know who's really in charge, so snooze with caution.

← **This little explorer, Jaguar, is a top-shelf kitten if we've ever seen one. Always up for an adventure, now he just needs to decide whether it's time for a nap in the canopy or to keep exploring the cat tunnels connecting new levels below.**

PURR POST

You've got to be kitten us! A fantastic purritecture design from Clark Nexsen and Oak City Customs, the Purr Post delivers a stylish accent piece for your living room while giving your cat new heights to explore. This design features different levels of fun for your cat, including a scratching post as its core. The wood slats are spaced purrfectly for any cat to get a paw through and shoo you away when you get too close. But the real fun starts at night, as this barkitecture comes alive with LEDs lighting up each layer, transforming it into a kitty rave stand with the push of a button. You could also use it as a nice floor lamp, but let's be honest; its best use is as a cat's personal laser show.

↑ As demonstrated here, your cat can find the ultimate vantage point or private sleeping quarters at the top of the Purr Post.

↑ **Built for the smallest, squishiest kittens, The Cat Arena awaits to provide snug comfort to any lucky cat.**

THE CAT ARENA

This cat design is inspired by nature and biomimicry, a design practice where form mimics designs found in nature to bring us closer to it. Team bioMEOWmicry from MHAworks looked at nesting structures of birds to create comfy spaces for your kitties to curl up in and get some peace and quiet. Crafted with felt pieces that fold, this cat den is spacious but small enough to feel comforting and cozy. The main compartment is hidden from view at the entrance, leaving just enough intrigue that'll tempt your curious feline to see what's inside. If you can't find your cat, our bet is they'll be in here having a quick nap before their 2 a.m. zoomies.

→ **This curly pup is happy to present the creators of the fabulous barkitectures you just read about!**

Meet the Barkitects and Rescues

As a thank-you to all the architects and rescues involved in this book, here's an index detailing all the people involved in the making of these doghouses and cathouses, including the rescues that Triangle Barkitecture partners with and the adoptable dogs and cats featured throughout.

BARKITECTS

Acrylick, 28
Cline Design Associates at https://www.clinedesignassoc.com/purpose/.
Team Members: Shawn Michael, Brett Powell, Kelly Strong, Whitney Sheppard, Kiersten Karch, Robert Sims.

bARC, 35
kasper architects + associates at https://www.kasperarch.com/.
Team Members: Jason Rivera, Vivian Chiang, Michael McKever, Kaylee Miller.

BARKitecture, 40
REdesign.build and REarchitecture at https://redesign.build/.
Team Members: Jeannine McAuliffe, Nicholas Hansman, Duncan Miller, Adam Windham, Zach Dawkins, Hilary Smith, Corey Eshelman, Bri Kaplan.

Barkside Bungalow, 48
Gensler at https://www.gensler.com/ and Oak City Customs at https://oakcitycustoms.com/.
Gensler Team Members: Anna Jensen, Lindsey Breitschwerdt, Adam Stoeckle,

Gianni Rodriguez, Brad Burns, Rob Allen, Oluwarotimi Osiberu, Andrew Levine, Sarah Smith, Rachel Baker, Cameron Westbrook, Maia Vexsler, Dustin Brugmann, David Gange.
Oak City Customs Team Members: Dylan Selinger, Chris Bednar.

Barkside Table, 32
IA Interior Architects supported by Laut Design at https://interiorarchitects.com/.
Team Members: Nicole Farmer, Nick Mosman, Marie Mosman.

Blueprint, 24
Integrated Design at https://id-pa.com/ and Lynch Mykins at https://lynchmykins.com/.
Integrated Design Team Members: Kristen Warring, Emmy Wood, Caitlyn Wilson, Hannah Atkinson, Tom Yount, Anya Aikman.
Lynch Mykins Team Members: Hannah Ross, Dale Osbon, Emily Flickinger.

BowHaus, 63
HagerSmith Design at https://hagersmith.com/.
Team Members: Jesse Reichmeider, Nick Troutman, Bryan Gibson, Sydney Roberts, and Trent Baker.

BowWow House, 77
RND Architects, PA at https://www.rndpa.com/.
Team Members: Led by Makenzie Morse with the help of Charles Nickelson, Rhonda Zack, Eric Wennerstrom, Anderson Puckett, Jennifer MacDonald.

Buddy Block, 34
Szostak Design and Szostak Build at https://szostakdesign.com/.
Team Members: Hari Vardhan, Joshua Gogan, Haifeng Liu, Olga Zakharova, Sarveswaran SP, Carolina Sarmiento Avila, Kali Faatz, Zac Szostak.

Build A Bark, 36
Studio 310 (formerly 310ai) at https://310.mainlandcreative.com/.
Team Members: Monica Carpenter, Austin Corriher, Baxter Wilson, Alex McMillan, Marlyn Stevenson, Allison Harris, Mayer Fabrics, PPG, Chamblis & Rabil Contractors.

Camp Barkitecture, 59
HH Architecture at https://hh-arch.com/.
Team Members: Laura Beesmer, Emily Barry, Siler Ransmeier, Trevor Cagle, Joanna Thomas, Elvis Cueva, Elizabeth Caliendo.

Cataritaville, 114
Veterinary Architecture Unleashed at https://veterinaryarchitectureunleashed.com/.
Team Members: Rhonda and Roger Layman.

Cat Flat, 120
RGG Architects at https://www.bhdp.com/ + Bull City Designs at https://www.bullcitydesigns.com/.
Team Members: Abe Uribe, James King, Harrison King.

Claw House, 129

CRB at https://www.crbgroup.com/.
Team Members: Felipe Lopera, Kristin Wimmer.

DOG-TON ARENA, 87

IA Interior Architects supported by BridgePoint General Contracting (see Barkside Table for company link).
Team Members: Nicole Farmer, Madelene Olsen, Melissa Carter.

Furigami, 93

IA Interior Architects supported by Atlantic Caseworks and Eno Company (see Barkside Table for company link).
Team Members: Nicole Farmer, Madelene Olsen.

HexaPawd, 38

LS3P at https://www.ls3p.com/ and Lynch Mykins (see Blueprint for company link).
LS3P Team Members: Jared Trussell, Jessica Lambert, Rebecca Eastwood, Felipe Lopera.
Lynch Mykins Team Members: James Leggett, Andrew Cook.

Hygge, 26

LS3P and Lynch Mykins (see HexaPawd and Blueprint for company links).
LS3P Team Members: John Calvert, Ethan Atherton, Felipe Lopera, Eileen McDonough, Julie Barghout.
Lynch Mykins Team Member: Taylor Mills.

Kattenhuis, 117

Hanbury at https://www.hanbury.design/.
Team Members: Carlie Gillespie, Sierra Hogan, Eliot Ball, Allison Harris.

Kitty Kubbies, 118

RND Architects, PA (see BowWow House for company link) with Davie Construction Co. at https://davieconstruction.com/.
Team Members: Led by Eric Wennerstrom with the help of Emily Currier, Makenzie Morse, Gauri Chalke, Jennifer MacDonald, Angellina Coats.

Lincoln Dogs, 89

Cline Design Associates (see Acrylick for company link).
Team Members: Brett Powell, Shawn Michael, Kelly Strong, Whitney Sheppard, Kiersten Karch, Arianna Sanchez, Brooke Grayson, Robert Sims, Tia Garrison.

North Carolina Museum of Bark, 67

BSA LifeStructures at https://www.bsalifestructures.com/.
Team Members: Timothy Stratton, Marc Metry, Sam Meyers, Kevin Hunt, Tyler Scire, Jeromy Clements, Kayli Mayne, Michael Deputy, Harsha Raju, Kasey Harrill, Vivian Chiang.

Oak Pawvilion, 80

kasper architects + associates (see bARC for company link).
Team Members: Vivian Chiang, Michael McKever, Dougald Fountain.

PAUSE & PAWS, 41

O'Brien Atkins Associates at https://www.obrienatkins.com/.
Team Members: Maria Jaramillo (Arch), Steven Harris (Arch), Kelly Wang (Land Arch), Alyssa Holland (Marketing), Darian Walker (Arch), Tim Hillhouse (Arch),

Stephany Luna (Arch), Nix Salcedo (Arch/LA), Weifen Yang (Arch), Michael Alligood (Elect. Eng).

Pawdenza, 29
Hanbury (see Kattenhuis for company link) with Brasfield & Gorrie at https://www.brasfieldgorrie.com/ and Unrefined Designs at https://www.unrefineddesigns.com/.
Hanbury Team Members: Chris Kwon, Erich Brunk, Kelly Clark, Albert Fajardo, Aishwarya Patil, Sarah Bannon, Nick Rossitch.
Brasfield & Gorrie Team Members: Grayson Hayter, Mitchell Hintz, Scott Cooper, Mattew Mottesheard, Christine Murtha, Giovanni Cavalotto, Amanda Brennan.
Unrefined Designs Team Member: Sal Recca.

Pawdular Shelving, 126
Arcadis at https://www.arcadis.com/.
Team Members: Tim Blanks, Nolan Markovich, Colin McCarville, Nic Kressman, Meet Bhayani, Marashi Patel, Emily Lewis, Daniel Floyd, Andrea Velosa, Meghan Weismiller, Bhalendu Gautam, Lauren Wallace, Debrashi Kedar, Lauren Scott.

Pawfee Table, 44
Clark Nexsen at https://www.clarknexsen.com/ and Raleigh Reclaimed at https://raleighreclaimed.com/.
Team Members: Trevor Healy, Caitlyn Schlaudecker, Will Pate, Tim Yang, Anna Traylor, Alex Cejka, Seiya Furukawa.
Raleigh Reclaimed Team Member: Corey Baughman.

Pawffee Table, 113
Szostak Design (see Buddy Block for company link).
Team Members: Phil Nelson, Hari Vardhan, Cassidy Putnam, Joshua Gogan, Haifeng Liu, Erin Craven.

PawGoda, 64
RGG Architects + Bull City Designs (see Cat Flat for company links).
Team Members: Abe Uribe, Sharon Pareja, Chadd Durant, James King.

PawPrairie Bench, 84
Tara Girolimon
Team Member: Tara Girolimon.

PawRabola, 98
Duda|Paine Architects, PA at https://www.dudapaine.com/.
Team Members: Chris Bitsas, Nick Hales, Evan McIver, Jack McManus, Ethan Porter, Shannon Robinson, Kyle Springer, Claire Zambrano.

PAWS, 30
CPL at https://cplteam.com/.
Team Members: Caroline Cox, Mitch Caldwell, Liz Caldwell, Finley.

Paws and Claws, 125
LS3P (see HexaPawd for company link) and Clancy & Theys at https://www.clancytheys.com/.
LS3P Team Members: Jared Trussell, Jessica Lambert, Rebecca Eastwood, Justin Acevedo, Bren Towle, Anthony Walke, Hunter Cutting, Oscar Avina-Rodriguez, Anna Epstein.
Clancy & Theys Team Members: David Lane, Stacey Coughlin, Erin Sherk.

Pawty Flight, 107

The Bobbitt Group, Inc. at https://www.bobbitt.com/.
Team Members: Robert Radcliffe, Keerti Javali, Kaitlyn Kelly, Kartini Divya, Brian Griffith, Jerry Fink, Dylan Hendley.

Pawvilion, 54

Gensler (see Barkside Bungalow for company link) and SEAS (Southeastern Architectural Systems) at https://seas-tr.com/.
Gensler Team Members: Anna Jensen, Lindsey Breitschwerdt, Adam Stoeckle, Gianni Rodriguez, Brad Burns, Rob Allen, Oluwarotimi Osiberu, Andrew Levine, Sarah Smith, Rachel Baker, Cameron Westbrook, Maia Vexsler, Dustin Brugmann, David Gange.
SEAS Team Members: Drew Rochester, Brad Armstrong, Timmy McCarthy.

PetShell, 66

ARCO Design/Build at https://arcodb.com/offices/raleigh-durham/.
Team Members: Ili Kafel, Josh Lamb, Regan Kind, Cole Shaffer.

Pooch Porch, 73

Clark Nexsen (see Pawfee Table for company link).
Team Members: Matt Bryan, Caitlyn Schlaudecker, Will Pate, Anna Traylor.

Pup Pawd, 69

kasper architects + associates (see bARC for company link).
Team Members: Jason Rivera, Vivian Chiang, Michael McKever, Julian Washington-McCoy.

Pup Side-Down, 102

BHDP Architecture (see Cat Flat for company link).
Team Members: Chelsea Walker, Christine Collins, Don Haunert, Emily Perry, Jori Durham, Kuhoo Patel, Michelle Lopez Orsini, Susmita Patil, William Alexander.

Purr Post, 132

Clark Nexsen and Oak City Customs (see Pawfee Table and Barkside Bungalow for company links).
Team Members: Trevor Healy, Caitlyn Schlaudecker, Will Pate, Tim Yang, Anna Traylor, Alex Cejka.

Retro Rover Retreat, 57

Habanero Architecture at https://www.habaneroarchitecture.com/ and Harken Construction at https://www.harkenconstruction.com/.
Team Members: Joe Lopez, design; Joe Apland Construction.

Rocket Cat, 123

Davis Kane Architects at https://www.daviskane.com/.
Team Members: Brittany Gagné, Jeremy Franklin, Hollie Mosher, Ryan Mlott, Vatsal Kesaria, Victoria White, Sheridan Young.

Rock'n Dog, 45

Knock on Wood by Enrique at https://knockonwoodbyenrique.com/.
Team Members: Enrique Anchorena, Romy Milla Paz.

RuffWave, 71

RGG Architects + Bull City Designs (see Cat Flat for company links).
Team Members: Abe Uribe, Sharon Pareja, Chadd Durant, Alex LeCroy, James King.

Step Paw-Sitin, 46

Clark Nexsen and Raleigh Reclaimed (see Pawfee Table for company links).
Team Members: Seiya Furukawa, Will Pate, Alex Cejka, Tim Yang, Anna Traylor.
Raleigh Reclaimed Team Member: Corey Baughman.

Summer Paw Cool, 83

Coffman Engineers, Inc. at https://www.coffman.com/.
Team Members: Lars Iverson, Joe Chang, Sean Sweeney, Lucas Lanham.

Tall Tails Bookshelf, 131

Moseley Architects at https://www.moseleyarchitects.com/.
Team Members: Ashely Dennis, Steve Nally, Jessica Hill, Shannon Morris, Melissa Almond, Shane Fogarty, Nicole Jeska, Ross Petersen, Brian Jones.

Tangled Tails House, 49

HDR, Inc. at https://www.hdrinc.com/.
Team Members: Kayli Marrano, Elaheh Houshmand, Nelson Reyes, Jake Hardin, Luke Brigman, Julio Martinez, Jenny Rhodus, Paul Forrest.

That's So Fetch, 53

Cline Design Associates (see Acrylick for company link).
Team Members: Michael Mesnard, Shawn Michael, Brett Powell, Whitney Sheppard, Kelly Strong, Martin Chavanne, Luis Guevara.

The Barker at the Purrserve, 42

Planworx Architecture at https://www.planworx.com/.
Team Members: Bob Naegele, Nick Strickland, Anya Aikman, Patricia Brezny, Casey Laborde.

The Bark Royal, 105

The Bobbitt Group, Inc. (see Pawty Flight for company link).
Team Members: Bailey Allred, Keerti Javali, Amy Bradley, Renee Rodriguez, Chris Pearson, Jordan Moore, Kartini Divya, Savannah Robin, Robert Radcliffe, Les Parker, Madeline Thompson, Dylan Hendley.

The Cat Arena, 133

MHAworks at https://www.mhaworks.com/.
Team Members: Fernando Zabala NCARB AIA CPD, Ally Gagliardo.

The Cat Credenza, 121

IA Interior Architects supported by Oak City Customs (see Barkside Table and Barkside Bungalow for company links).
Team Members: Nicole Farmer, Jessica Veil-Dewitt, Melissa Carter, Mallory Koerner.

The Furbonacci Table, 101

Planworx Architecture (see The Barker at the Purrserve for company link).
Team Members: Justin Johnson, Tara Stowell, Ashlyn Tolman, Casey Braun, Nick Strickland, Bob Naegele.

The Mutt Hutt, 78
Moseley Architects (see Tall Tails Bookshelf for company link).
Team Members: Ashley Dennis, Melissa Almond, Steve Nally, Jessica Hill, Shannon Morris, John Nichols.

The Nut House, 23
Redline Design Group at https://www.redlinedg.com/ and Unrefined Designs at https://www.unrefineddesigns.com/.
Team Members: Salvatore Recca, Todd Wilson, Erich Brunk, Katie Briggs, Emily Bargy, Toyin Adebiyi, Elisa Christopher, Emilie Krysa, Patricia Chenery.

The Transformation Station, 97
Summit Design and Engineering Services at https://summitde.com/.
Team Members: Marissa Mondin, Juan Osorio, Stephanie Seifert, Vitaliia Matiiuk Basteri.

The Woof Wagon, 58
Apogee Consulting Group at https://www.acg-pa.com/ and BZ Construction at https://bzconstruction.us/.
Team Members: Jeff Brooks (Team Leader), Steve Beezley, Mac Harmon, Cailey Kurkul, King Choy, Sam Crawford, Kyle Genther, Ben Wolfman, Brian Needham, Dana Case, Deonna Dalton-Brooks.

T.L.C., 60
HH Architecture (see Camp Barkitecture for company link).
Team Members: Jackson Kiel, Morgan Bryant, Siler Ransmeier, Eric Mura, Cassidy Putnam.

Ultimutt Hut, 25
Studio 310 (formerly 310ai) (see Build A Bark for company link).
Team Members: Albert M. McDonald, Alex McMillan, Caila Bridges, Adriane Field, Kelly Janca, Clark Williamson, 3Form, Casalis Habitat Matter.

Wagon Tails, 100
Kilian Engineering, Inc. at https://www.kilianengineering.com/.
Team Members: Barry Frazier, Greg Taylor, Jehnny Braswell, Erika Bogue, Sheyla Torres, Cody Gardner, Brandon Lawrence.

Whole-Leash It, 82
Hanbury (see Kattenhuis for company link) with Barringer Construction at https://www.barringerconstruction.com/.
Hanbury Team Members: Amelia Murphy, Nick Rossitch, Julie Barghout.
Barringer Construction Team Members: Carlie Wallin, Lauren Reahard.

Who Let the KONG Out!, 108
The Bobbitt Group, Inc. (see Pawty Flight for company link).
Team Members: Bailey Allred, Renee Rodriguez, Amy Bradley, Amber Jones, Ashley Kersey, Lizette Anderson, Dylan Hendley.

Woofstock, 95
Planworx Architecture (see The Barker at the Purrserve for company link).
Team Members: Parker Smith, Brad Williams, Casey Laborde, Casey Braun, Kaleigh Gamsey Laborde.

RESCUES

Change of Heart Pit Bull Rescue at https://www.cohpbr.org/.
Rescue dog featured: Peony (67).

Connie's Kittens at http://www.connieskittens.org/.
Rescue cats featured: Bentley (110), Tofu (121), Dakota (118, 119), Gimli (122, 123, 126), Everest (128), Bruno (128, 129), and Ferrari (124).

Freedom Ride Rescue at https://www.freedom-ride.org/.
Rescue animals featured: Michelle Myers (12, 25), Benjamin Barker (54), and Granola (98).

Friends of Wake County Animal Center at https://www.friendsofwakeanimals.org/.
Rescue dog featured: Santanna (29).

Hope Animal Rescue at https://hoperescues.org/.
Rescue animals featured: Babushka Anya (16, 77), Archie (24), The Barker at the Purrserve (42), Hiccup (53), and Firefly (26).

Meow House Cat Rescue at https://www.meowhousecatrescue.com/.

Paw Prints Animal Rescue at https://pawprintsrescue.org/.

Peak Lab Rescue at https://www.peaklabrescue.com/.

Saving Grace Animals for Adoption at https://savinggracenc.org/.

Triangle Beagle Rescue at https://www.tribeagles.org/.
Rescue dogs featured: Puck (57), Pawty Flight (107), and Who Let the KONG Out! (108).

SPECIAL THANKS

To Shawna and our furry family. To Maya and Savannah for being my inspiration, and Scotch, Stormi, Julip, Brandy, Goose, and Penelope for helping us realize that pet rescue is hard work and adopting them out is even harder.

To my mom and dad, for introducing me to the love of pets early on and the positive impact they have in our lives.

To our amazing committee and volunteers that bring this event to life: Dr. Shawna Varichak, Dharshyani and Jon Jackson, Anne Lebo, Megan Kaufman, Vivian Chiang, Lindsay Elliot, Brittany Larsen, Jamie Bailey, Miyuki Keller, Noelle Robinson, and Scott and Alex Krabath.

To AIA Triangle and all the amazing local architects and designers that continually surprise me with their endless creativity and pushing design.

To all rescues, everywhere, for their commitment and tireless efforts in helping our pet population around the world.

ABOUT THE AUTHOR

Joshua Thomasson is a passionate pet lover, architect, designer, and advocate for community engagement. After growing up in the small town of Danville, VA, Joshua has had the privilege of traveling the world, experiencing firsthand the profound impact that design can have on communities and cultures. A proud graduate of Virginia Tech, Joshua's commitment to community outreach is evident through his involvement with various programs, notably serving as president of Barkitecture. Since its inaugural event in 2019, Joshua has been chairman of the Triangle Barkitecture competition sponsored by AIA Triangle, where he has also served on the board of directors. Instilled with a love of pets from an early age, Joshua is dedicated to bringing the joy and companionship of pets to as many people as possible.

ABOUT THE PHOTOGRAPHER

Alyssa Stepien is an art director, graphic designer, and photographer living in Raleigh, NC. Inspired by her first two rescue dogs, Oliver and Junebug, in 2016 she began volunteering with animal rescue organizations in the area. She soon realized how important quality photos are in getting foster pets noticed by potential adopters. In order to help, she learned photography and founded Rose + Anchor Photography with the goal of photographing as many adoptable pets as possible. She believes that everyone should find their volunteer passion (whatever it is!), and she is truly grateful that she has the privilege and skills to help animals in this way. Alyssa has been the photographer for Triangle Barkitecture since its inaugural event in 2019.

First published in 2025 by Rock Point, an imprint of The Quarto Group,
142 West 36th Street, 4th Floor, New York, NY 10018, USA
(212) 779-4972 www.Quarto.com

Rock Point titles are also available at discount for retail, wholesale, promotional,
and bulk purchase. For details, contact the Special Sales Manager by email at
specialsales@quarto.com or by mail at The Quarto Group, Attn: Special Sales
Manager, 100 Cummings Center, Suite 265D, Beverly, MA 01915 USA.

10 9 8 7 6 5 4 3 2 1

ISBN: 978-1-57715-533-1

Digital edition published in 2025
eISBN: 978-0-7603-9662-9

Library of Congress Control Number: 2025931419

Group Publisher: Rage Kindelsperger
Editorial Director: Erin Canning
Creative Director: Laura Drew
Managing Editor: Cara Donaldson
Editor: Katelynn Abraham
Cover and Interior Design: Simon Larkin

Printed in China